MASTERING THE

COMMODITY MARKET

STRATEGIES FOR SUCCESS

by

Lalit Mohanty

Table of Contents:

Chapter 1: Introduction to Commodity Markets

- What Are Commodity Markets?
- The History of Commodity Trading
- Types of Commodities
- Why Trade in the Commodity Market?

Chapter 2: Understanding Commodities

- Classification of Commodities
- Physical vs. Financial Commodities
- Supply and Demand Dynamics
- Factors Affecting Commodity Prices

Chapter 3: Market Participants

- The Commodity Market Ecosystem
- Major Players: Producers, Consumers, Speculators, and Hedgers
- Role of Brokers, Exchanges, and Regulators

Chapter 4: Commodity Market Instruments

- Spot vs. Futures Markets
- Options, Swaps, and Forwards

- Trend Following Strategies

- Mean Reversion Strategies

- Carry Trades and Spread Trading

- Seasonal and Calendar Spread Strategies

Chapter 9: Trading Psychology

- Emotions and Trading

- Discipline and Patience

- Developing a Winning Mindset

- Learning from Mistakes

Chapter 10: Commodity Market Research

- Staying Informed: News Sources and Reports

- Historical Data and Analysis

- Economic and Political Research

- Staying Ahead of Market Trends

Chapter 11: Trading Systems and Automation

- Algorithmic Trading

- Trading Software and Platforms

- Backtesting and Optimization

- Risk Management in Automated Trading

Chapter 12: Commodity Market Ethics and Regulations

- Insider Trading and Market Manipulation

- Regulatory Bodies and Oversight

- Compliance and Reporting Requirements

- Legal and Ethical Considerations

Chapter 13: Commodity Market Strategies for Beginners

- Getting Started with a Simulated Account

- Paper Trading and Building Experience

- Creating a Trading Plan

- Selecting Your First Trades

Chapter 14: Advanced Trading Strategies

- Scalping and Day Trading

- Swing Trading and Position Trading

- Options and Derivatives Strategies

- Quantitative Analysis

Chapter 15: Case Studies and Real-Life Examples

- Successful Commodity Traders

- Notable Market Crashes and Recoveries

- Lessons from Historical Events

INDEX

"Mastering the Commodity Market: Strategies for Success" aims to provide readers with a comprehensive guide to understanding and successfully navigating the complex world of commodity trading. Whether you are a novice looking to enter the market or an experienced trader seeking to refine your strategies, this book equips you with the knowledge and tools necessary to thrive in the world of commodities.

CHAPTER 1

INTRODUCTION TO COMMODITY MARKETS

The world of commodity markets represents a dynamic and essential facet of the global economy. Commodity trading serves as the bedrock of various industries, influencing everything from agriculture and energy to precious metals and currencies. In this chapter, we delve into the fundamental aspects that define commodity markets, tracing their historical roots, exploring the diverse array of commodities traded, and understanding the motivations behind engaging in commodity trading.

What Are Commodity Markets?

Commodity markets are platforms where raw materials, primary goods, and tangible assets are bought and sold.

These markets facilitate the exchange of physical goods or standardized contracts representing these goods. Participants in commodity markets include producers, consumers, speculators, and hedgers, each contributing to the market's vibrancy and liquidity.

Unlike financial markets that primarily involve stocks, bonds, or currencies, commodity markets deal with tangible assets such as agricultural products (e.g., wheat, corn), energy resources (e.g., crude oil, natural gas), metals (e.g., gold, copper), and more. The physical nature of commodities makes these markets unique, as the goods traded have intrinsic value and are subject to the forces of supply and demand.

The History of Commodity Trading

The roots of commodity trading can be traced back centuries, with historical records revealing the existence of organized markets for the exchange of goods. Early civilizations engaged in barter systems, exchanging surplus crops, livestock, and other commodities to meet their needs.

As societies evolved, so did the mechanisms for trading commodities. The emergence of commodity exchanges in the 19th and 20th centuries marked a significant shift. These exchanges provided centralized platforms where buyers and sellers could come together to establish prices and execute trades. Over time, commodities trading became more sophisticated, incorporating futures contracts, options, and other financial instruments to manage risk and enhance market efficiency.

Types of Commodities

Commodities can be broadly categorized into two main types: hard commodities and soft commodities. Hard commodities include natural resources like metals, energy resources, and minerals. Soft commodities encompass agricultural products, including crops and livestock. Each category is further divided into specific commodities, creating a diverse market with a wide range of assets for trading.

Understanding these distinctions is crucial for market participants, as different commodities exhibit unique price drivers, supply-demand dynamics, and risk factors. Moreover, the classification influences the trading strategies and considerations for each type of commodity.

Why Trade in the Commodity Market?

Trading in commodity markets offers a plethora of opportunities and benefits for various market participants. Producers can use these markets to hedge against price volatility, ensuring a stable income for their goods. Consumers, on the other hand, can secure a predictable supply of essential resources. Speculators aim to profit from price movements, while investors diversify their portfolios by including commodities as an asset class.

Commodity markets also play a vital role in global economic stability. Prices established in these markets influence production decisions, impact inflation rates, and contribute to overall market efficiency. As the interconnectedness of the global economy continues to grow, understanding and participating in commodity markets become increasingly important for individuals and institutions alike.

In the subsequent chapters, we will delve deeper into the intricacies of commodity trading, exploring the various instruments available, analyzing market dynamics, and providing strategies for success in this dynamic and essential sector of the financial world.

CHAPTER 2

UNDERSTANDING COMMODITIES

In the pursuit of mastering the commodity market, a fundamental comprehension of the commodities themselves is imperative. This chapter will explore the intricacies of commodities, their classifications, and the dynamic forces that drive their markets. From the basic division between hard and soft commodities to the influences of supply and demand, we will unravel the layers that make commodities a unique and compelling asset class.

Classification of Commodities

Commodities can be broadly categorized into two main types: hard commodities and soft commodities.

- *Hard Commodities:* These encompass natural resources that are typically mined or extracted. Metals like gold, silver, copper, and energy resources such as crude oil and natural gas fall under this category. The value of hard commodities is often influenced by industrial demand, geopolitical factors, and global economic trends.

- *Soft Commodities:* This category includes agricultural products, ranging from crops like wheat, corn, and soybeans to livestock such as cattle and pork. Soft commodities are significantly influenced by weather conditions, agricultural practices, and geopolitical events that can impact the production and distribution of these goods.

Understanding the distinctions between hard and soft commodities is essential for market participants, as each category responds differently to market forces and external factors.

Physical vs. Financial Commodities

Another crucial differentiation lies between physical and financial commodities.

- *Physical Commodities:* These are tangible goods that are bought and sold in their actual form. Physical commodities involve the transfer of ownership from one party to another, and the goods can be delivered physically. Examples include barrels of oil, bushels of wheat, or ounces of gold.

- *Financial Commodities:* In contrast, financial commodities are represented by contracts, such as futures or options, which derive their value from the underlying physical commodity. These financial instruments provide exposure to price movements without the need for physical delivery. Traders and investors often engage in financial commodities for speculative purposes or risk management.

Supply and Demand Dynamics

The forces of supply and demand play a central role in determining commodity prices. The delicate balance between the availability of a commodity (supply) and the desire for that commodity (demand) establishes its market value.

- *Supply Factors:* Natural disasters, geopolitical events, technological advancements, and government policies can influence the production and availability of commodities. For example, a drought affecting major wheat-producing regions can lead to a reduction in wheat supply, causing prices to rise.

- *Demand Factors:* Economic growth, population trends, and shifts in consumer behavior impact the demand for commodities. Industrialization in emerging markets, for instance, can drive the demand for metals and energy resources, affecting their prices.

Understanding these supply and demand dynamics is essential for traders and investors seeking to navigate commodity markets successfully.

Factors Affecting Commodity Prices

Commodity prices are influenced by a myriad of factors that extend beyond supply and demand dynamics. In this section, we explore some key elements that can significantly impact commodity prices:

- *Geopolitical Events:* Political instability, trade tensions, and conflicts can disrupt the production and distribution of commodities, leading to price volatility.

- *Weather Conditions:* Natural phenomena such as droughts, floods, hurricanes, and extreme temperatures can affect agricultural production, impacting prices in the soft commodity markets.

- *Economic Indicators:* Economic data, such as GDP growth, inflation rates, and employment figures, can provide insights into overall economic health and impact the demand for various commodities.

- *Currency Movements:* As commodities are globally traded, fluctuations in currency values can influence their prices. A weaker currency can make commodities more attractive to international buyers.

In the subsequent chapters, we will delve deeper into the specific characteristics of different types of commodities, examining their unique market dynamics and exploring strategies for analyzing and trading these assets.

CHAPTER 3

MARKET PARTICIPANTS

In the vast and intricate landscape of commodity markets, a multitude of participants engages in diverse roles, collectively shaping the dynamics of these markets. This chapter will dissect the ecosystem of the commodity market, identifying key players and elucidating the roles they play. From producers and consumers to speculators and hedgers, and the pivotal functions of brokers, exchanges, and regulators, we will navigate through the complex network that constitutes the commodity trading world.

The Commodity Market Ecosystem

The commodity market functions as a dynamic ecosystem where various participants interact, each contributing to the market's liquidity, efficiency, and vibrancy. Understanding the roles of these participants is essential for grasping the intricacies of commodity trading.

At the heart of this ecosystem are the primary actors: producers, consumers, speculators, and hedgers. These participants bring diverse perspectives, motivations, and strategies to the market, creating a dynamic interplay of forces.

Major Players: Producers, Consumers, Speculators, and Hedgers

- *Producers:* Producers are entities involved in the extraction, cultivation, or manufacturing of commodities. This category includes farmers, miners, and energy companies. Producers often use commodity markets to hedge against price volatility, ensuring a stable income for their products.

- *Consumers:* On the flip side, consumers are entities that utilize commodities as inputs for their operations. Manufacturers, energy consumers, and agricultural processors fall into this category. Consumers engage in commodity markets to secure a reliable supply of necessary resources at predictable prices.

- *Speculators:* Speculators are individuals or institutions that seek to profit from price fluctuations in commodity markets. They do not have a direct interest in the physical delivery of the commodity but aim to capitalize on market movements. Speculators add liquidity to the market and provide an essential counterbalance to hedgers.

- *Hedgers:* Hedgers use commodity markets to manage the risk associated with price volatility. These participants aim to protect themselves from adverse price movements by entering into positions that offset their exposure. For example, a wheat farmer might hedge against falling prices by selling futures contracts.

Understanding the motivations and strategies of these major players is crucial for comprehending the market dynamics and anticipating potential shifts.

Role of Brokers, Exchanges, and Regulators

- *Brokers:* Brokers act as intermediaries, facilitating the execution of trades between buyers and sellers. They can be individuals, firms, or online platforms that connect market participants. Brokers provide valuable services such as order execution, market research, and trading advice. The choice of a broker can significantly impact a trader's experience and success in the commodity market.

- *Exchanges:* Commodity exchanges are centralized platforms where buyers and sellers come together to trade standardized contracts. These exchanges provide transparency, liquidity, and a regulated environment for market participants. Examples of major commodity exchanges include the Chicago Mercantile Exchange (CME), the London Metal Exchange (LME), and the Intercontinental Exchange (ICE).

- *Regulators:* Regulatory bodies play a crucial role in overseeing and maintaining the integrity of commodity markets. They establish rules and regulations to ensure fair and transparent trading practices. Regulatory oversight helps prevent fraud, manipulation, and other unethical activities that could compromise market integrity. Different countries have regulatory authorities responsible for overseeing commodity markets and ensuring compliance with applicable laws.

The synergy among producers, consumers, speculators, hedgers, brokers, exchanges, and regulators creates a robust and well-functioning commodity market. In the subsequent chapters, we will delve into the specific roles of each participant, exploring their strategies, motivations, and the impact they have on commodity market dynamics.

CHAPTER 4

COMMODITY MARKET INSTRUMENTS

In the intricate tapestry of commodity markets, a myriad of financial instruments provides participants with diverse avenues for trading, hedging, and speculating. This chapter will illuminate the various instruments available in commodity markets, differentiating between spot and futures markets, exploring options, swaps, and forwards, and elucidating the distinctions between exchange-traded and over-the-counter (OTC) contracts. Additionally, we will guide readers on how to navigate this plethora of instruments and choose the right one based on their trading objectives and risk tolerance.

Spot vs. Futures Markets

- *Spot Markets:* In spot markets, commodities are bought and sold for immediate delivery and payment.

These transactions involve the physical exchange of the commodity. Spot markets provide real-time pricing and immediate ownership transfer, making them essential for producers and consumers looking for immediate transactions and physical delivery of the commodity.

- *Futures Markets:* Futures markets, on the other hand, involve contracts for the future delivery of a commodity at a predetermined price. These standardized contracts are traded on commodity exchanges and are used for both speculative and hedging purposes. Futures contracts allow participants to gain exposure to price movements without the need for immediate physical delivery.

Understanding the distinction between spot and futures markets is crucial for market participants as it influences the trading strategies and considerations for each.

Options, Swaps, and Forwards

- *Options:* Commodity options provide the holder with the right (but not the obligation) to buy or sell a specified amount of a commodity at a predetermined price within a specified time frame. Options offer flexibility for hedging and speculating, allowing participants to manage risk or capitalize on market movements.

- *Swaps:* Swaps involve the exchange of cash flows between two parties based on the price movements of a commodity. Unlike futures contracts, swaps do not require an upfront exchange of assets. Commodity swaps can be customized to meet the specific needs of the parties involved, making them versatile instruments for managing risk and exposure.

- *Forwards:* Forwards are customized contracts between two parties to buy or sell a specific quantity of a commodity at an agreed-upon price at a future date. Unlike futures contracts, forwards are not standardized and are traded over-the-counter. Forwards are often used for hedging purposes, allowing participants to lock in prices for future transactions.

Each of these instruments serves distinct purposes, and their suitability depends on the specific objectives and risk tolerance of market participants.

Exchange-Traded vs. Over-The-Counter (OTC) Contracts

- *Exchange-Traded Contracts:* These contracts are standardized and traded on organized exchanges, providing transparency, liquidity, and a regulated environment. Exchange-traded contracts, such as futures and options, are characterized by clear terms and are subject to the rules and regulations of the exchange.

- *Over-The-Counter (OTC) Contracts:* OTC contracts are customized agreements negotiated directly between two parties. These contracts are not traded on organized exchanges, offering greater flexibility but often requiring more in-depth negotiations. OTC contracts, including swaps and forwards, are tailored to the specific needs of the participants.

Choosing between exchange-traded and OTC contracts depends on factors such as market access, liquidity requirements, and the need for customization.

How to Choose the Right Instrument

Selecting the right instrument in the commodity market is a crucial decision that depends on various factors:

- *Risk Tolerance:* Consider your risk tolerance and the level of exposure you are comfortable with. Different instruments carry varying degrees of risk, and understanding your risk appetite is essential.

- *Objective of Trading:* Clarify your trading objective. Are you looking to hedge against price volatility, speculate on price movements, or invest for the long term? Different instruments align with different trading goals.

- *Market Conditions:* Assess the prevailing market conditions. Volatile markets may be suitable for options trading, while more stable markets might favor the use of futures contracts for hedging.

- *Liquidity:* Evaluate the liquidity of the instrument. More liquid instruments, such as exchange-traded futures, can offer easier entry and exit points for trades.

- *Regulatory Considerations:* Be aware of regulatory considerations. Some instruments are subject to specific regulations, and understanding these regulations is crucial for compliance.

By carefully considering these factors, market participants can make informed decisions on which instruments align best with their trading objectives and risk profile. In the subsequent chapters, we will delve into specific strategies for trading each type of commodity instrument, providing a comprehensive guide for mastering the intricacies of commodity markets.

CHAPTER 5

FUNDAMENTAL ANALYSIS

In the intricate world of commodity markets, the ability to conduct effective fundamental analysis is a cornerstone of success. This chapter will delve into the nuances of fundamental analysis, a method that involves evaluating the underlying factors that drive commodity prices. From understanding supply and demand fundamentals to navigating the impacts of weather, politics, and geopolitical events, and deciphering government reports and economic indicators along with commodity-specific metrics, we will equip traders with the tools to make informed decisions in the dynamic commodity market landscape.

Analyzing Supply and Demand Fundamentals

Central to fundamental analysis is a thorough examination of supply and demand dynamics. This involves scrutinizing factors that influence the production and consumption of commodities.

- *Supply Factors:* Assessing the factors that affect the supply side involves considering production levels, technological advancements, geopolitical stability, and weather conditions. For example, a disruption in oil production due to geopolitical tensions can significantly impact the supply of crude oil, affecting prices.

- *Demand Factors:* Understanding demand is equally crucial. Economic growth, population trends, and shifts in consumer behavior can influence the demand for commodities. For instance, a booming economy may lead to increased demand for industrial metals, affecting their prices.

Weather, Politics, and Geopolitical Events

Commodities are inherently vulnerable to external forces such as weather patterns, political decisions, and geopolitical events.

- *Weather:* Weather conditions play a pivotal role in the agricultural sector. Crop yields can be heavily influenced by factors like droughts, floods, and extreme temperatures. Traders need to stay abreast of weather forecasts and patterns to anticipate potential impacts on supply and prices.

- *Politics:* Political decisions, regulations, and trade policies can significantly affect commodity markets. Elections, changes in government, and geopolitical tensions can introduce uncertainty, leading to price volatility.

- *Geopolitical Events:* Events on the global stage, such as conflicts, sanctions, or diplomatic tensions, can disrupt the production and distribution of commodities. Traders must monitor geopolitical developments to gauge potential market impacts.

Government Reports and Economic Indicators

Government reports and economic indicators provide valuable insights into the overall economic health and specific sectors relevant to commodity markets.

- *Government Reports:* Reports from government agencies, such as the U.S. Department of Agriculture (USDA) for agricultural commodities or the Energy Information Administration (EIA) for energy resources, offer crucial data on production, inventories, and consumption. Traders often analyze these reports to gauge market conditions.

- *Economic Indicators:* Broad economic indicators, including GDP growth, inflation rates, and employment figures, can influence the demand for commodities. A growing economy may stimulate demand, while economic contraction may lead to reduced consumption.

Commodity-Specific Metrics

Each commodity has unique characteristics and metrics that impact its market dynamics. Traders should be familiar with commodity-specific metrics to make informed decisions.

- *Energy Commodities:* For energy commodities like oil and natural gas, metrics such as production levels, inventories, and global demand are crucial. Additionally, geopolitical events in oil-producing regions can have a significant impact on energy prices.

- *Agricultural Commodities:* Crop reports, weather forecasts, and planting and harvesting data are vital for analyzing agricultural commodities. Traders must also consider factors like disease outbreaks and trade agreements that can affect the supply and demand for agricultural products.

- *Metals:* Industrial metals, such as copper and aluminum, are sensitive to economic indicators like manufacturing data and infrastructure development. Precious metals like gold and silver, on the other hand, may respond to inflation concerns and geopolitical uncertainties.

Incorporating these fundamental analysis techniques into trading strategies empowers participants to navigate the complexity of commodity markets. In the subsequent chapters, we will explore technical analysis, risk management, and trading strategies, providing a comprehensive guide for mastering the art of commodity trading.

CHAPTER 6

TECHNICAL ANALYSIS

In the dynamic and fast-paced world of commodity trading, technical analysis stands as a powerful tool for deciphering market trends and making informed decisions. This chapter will explore the basics of technical analysis, delving into the significance of price charts and patterns, the application of technical indicators, and the strategic integration of both fundamental and technical analysis for a comprehensive approach to commodity market analysis.

Basics of Technical Analysis

Technical analysis is a method of evaluating and predicting price movements based on historical price data. It operates on the premise that historical price movements and patterns tend to repeat, allowing traders to identify potential future trends.

- *Market Psychology:* At its core, technical analysis reflects market psychology. It recognizes that market participants' emotions and behaviors are often reflected in price movements. By analyzing historical price charts, traders aim to discern patterns that may indicate future price directions.

- *Price Discounts Everything:* Technical analysts believe that all relevant information, including market fundamentals and external factors, is already reflected in the price. Therefore, they focus on studying price movements and patterns to make predictions.

- *History Tends to Repeat Itself:* One of the foundational principles of technical analysis is that historical price patterns and trends have a tendency to repeat. Traders use this principle to identify potential entry and exit points for their positions.

Price Charts and Patterns

- *Candlestick Charts:* Candlestick charts are widely used in technical analysis. They provide information about the opening, closing, high, and low prices for a specific period. Candlestick patterns, such as doji, engulfing, and hammer, offer insights into potential trend reversals or continuations.

- *Support and Resistance:* Support and resistance levels are key concepts in technical analysis. Support is a price level at which a commodity tends to stop falling, while resistance is a level at which it tends to stop rising. These levels help traders identify potential entry and exit points.

- *Chart Patterns:* Technical analysts study chart patterns to identify potential trend reversals or continuations. Common patterns include head and shoulders, triangles, and flags. Recognizing these patterns can aid traders in making strategic decisions.

Technical Indicators

- *Moving Averages:* Moving averages smooth out price data to create a single flowing line, allowing traders to identify trends over a specified period. The intersection of short-term and long-term moving averages can signal potential trend changes.

- *Relative Strength Index (RSI):* RSI measures the magnitude of recent price changes to evaluate overbought or oversold conditions. It is displayed as an oscillator that ranges from 0 to 100. An RSI above 70 may indicate overbought conditions, while an RSI below 30 may suggest oversold conditions.

- *Moving Average Convergence Divergence (MACD):* MACD is a trend-following momentum indicator that shows the relationship between two moving averages of a security's price. Traders look for crossovers and divergences in the MACD to identify potential trend changes.

Combining Fundamental and Technical Analysis

While fundamental analysis provides insights into the underlying factors influencing commodity prices, technical analysis offers a real-time view of market sentiment and potential trend directions. Combining these two approaches can provide traders with a more comprehensive understanding of the market.

- *Confirmation of Trends:* Fundamental analysis can confirm or challenge the trends identified through technical analysis. For example, if technical analysis suggests an uptrend in oil prices, fundamental factors such as geopolitical tensions or changes in production levels can provide confirmation.

- *Timing Entries and Exits:* Technical analysis can help traders time their entries and exits based on historical price patterns and indicators. Fundamental analysis, meanwhile, can guide traders in understanding the broader market context and potential catalysts for price movements.

- *Risk Management:* The combination of fundamental and technical analysis enables traders to implement effective risk management strategies. By understanding the broader market fundamentals and using technical tools to identify potential turning points, traders can optimize their risk-reward ratios.

In conclusion, mastering technical analysis involves a deep understanding of price charts, patterns, and technical indicators. When integrated with fundamental analysis, traders can develop a well-rounded approach to navigating the complexities of commodity markets. In the subsequent chapters, we will explore risk management strategies and various trading techniques, providing a comprehensive guide for successful commodity trading.

CHAPTER 7

RISK MANAGEMENT

In the dynamic and unpredictable realm of commodity trading, successful market participants recognize the paramount importance of effective risk management. This chapter will explore the various types of risks inherent in commodity markets, delve into strategies for mitigating these risks, and emphasize the significance of disciplined risk management in ensuring long-term success.

Types of Risks in Commodity Trading

- *Price Risk:* The most apparent risk in commodity trading is price risk. Prices can fluctuate due to various factors, such as changes in supply and demand, geopolitical events, and economic indicators. Traders face the constant challenge of predicting and adapting to these price movements.

- *Market Risk:* Market risk encompasses the broader risk of adverse market movements. This includes volatility, liquidity risk, and the risk of market shocks triggered by unforeseen events. Traders must be prepared for sudden and unexpected changes in market conditions.

- *Leverage Risk:* The use of leverage amplifies both potential gains and losses. While leverage can enhance profits, it also increases the risk of significant losses. Traders need to carefully manage their leverage to avoid excessive exposure.

- *Operational Risk:* Operational risk involves the potential for losses due to inadequate systems, human error, or technical failures. Traders must implement robust operational processes and risk controls to mitigate these challenges.

Using Stop Loss Orders and Limit Orders

- *Stop Loss Orders:* A stop loss order is a risk management tool that allows traders to set a predetermined price at which their position will be automatically sold to limit potential losses. This order helps traders maintain discipline and prevent emotional decision-making during market fluctuations.

- *Limit Orders:* Limit orders are used to lock in profits by automatically selling a position when the commodity reaches a specified profit level. This order type enables traders to secure gains and avoid the temptation to hold onto positions for too long.

Diversification Strategies

Diversification is a fundamental risk management strategy that involves spreading investments across different assets or commodities. By diversifying, traders reduce the impact of poor performance in one commodity on their overall portfolio. This strategy aims to achieve a balance between risk and reward.

Managing Leverage

While leverage can magnify profits, it also amplifies the potential for losses. Effective risk management involves judiciously using leverage, considering factors such as account size, risk tolerance, and market conditions. Traders should avoid excessive leverage that could lead to margin calls and significant financial setbacks.

Position Sizing and Portfolio Management

Determining the appropriate size for each position, known as position sizing, is a critical aspect of risk management. Traders should calculate position sizes based on their account size, risk tolerance, and the volatility of the commodity being traded. Additionally, effective portfolio management involves monitoring the overall risk exposure across all positions to avoid overconcentration in a single commodity or market.

Adapting to Changing Market Conditions

Market conditions are dynamic and can evolve rapidly. Successful risk management requires the ability to adapt to changing circumstances. Traders should regularly reassess their risk exposure, adjust position sizes, and update risk management strategies based on shifts in market dynamics.

The Importance of Discipline and Patience

Discipline and patience are foundational principles in risk management. Emotional reactions to market fluctuations can lead to impulsive decisions that undermine risk management strategies. By maintaining discipline and patience, traders are better equipped to stick to their risk management plans and navigate the inherent uncertainties of commodity markets.

In conclusion, risk management is a fundamental aspect of successful commodity trading. Traders must be proactive in identifying and mitigating risks, using tools such as stop loss orders, diversification, and prudent leverage. By incorporating these strategies and maintaining discipline, market participants can enhance their resilience and longevity in the dynamic world of commodity trading. In the subsequent chapters, we will explore advanced trading strategies and delve into the psychological aspects of trading.

CHAPTER 8

TRADING STRATEGIES

In the ever-evolving landscape of commodity markets, employing effective trading strategies is essential for navigating the complexities and capitalizing on opportunities. This chapter explores various trading strategies tailored to the unique characteristics of commodity trading. From trend following and mean reversion to carry trades, spread trading, and seasonal/calendar spread strategies, each approach offers a distinct methodology for achieving success in the dynamic commodity market.

Trend Following Strategies

Trend following strategies are based on the premise that once a trend is established, it is likely to persist. Traders employing trend following strategies seek to identify and capitalize on existing market trends. Key elements of trend following strategies include:

- *Moving Averages:* Traders often use moving averages to identify trends by smoothing out price data over a specific period. Crossovers between short-term and long-term moving averages can signal the beginning or end of a trend.

- *Trendlines:* Trendlines help traders visualize the direction of a trend by connecting the lows or highs in a price chart. Breakouts or breakdowns from these trendlines can indicate potential trend reversals or continuations.

- *Momentum Indicators:* Momentum indicators like the Relative Strength Index (RSI) or Moving Average Convergence Divergence (MACD) are used to confirm the strength of a trend. Overbought or oversold conditions may signal potential trend exhaustion.

Mean Reversion Strategies

Mean reversion strategies are based on the idea that prices tend to revert to their historical average over time. Traders employing mean reversion strategies look for opportunities to profit from price deviations from the average. Key elements of mean reversion strategies include:

- *Bollinger Bands:* Bollinger Bands help identify overbought or oversold conditions by displaying price volatility. When prices deviate significantly from the bands, traders may anticipate a reversion to the mean.

- *Statistical Indicators:* Traders may use statistical measures such as standard deviations to identify price extremes. When prices deviate from the historical average by a certain number of standard deviations, mean reversion traders may anticipate a correction.

Carry Trades and Spread Trading

- *Carry Trades:* Carry trades involve capitalizing on the interest rate differentials between currencies or commodities. Traders can earn interest by holding a high-yielding commodity or currency while simultaneously borrowing or selling a lower-yielding one.

- *Spread Trading:* Spread trading involves simultaneously buying and selling related contracts to profit from changes in the price difference between them. For example, traders may go long on one crude oil contract and short on another, aiming to profit from changes in the spread between the two.

Seasonal and Calendar Spread Strategies

- *Seasonal Strategies:* Seasonal trading strategies involve exploiting recurring patterns or trends that occur during specific seasons. For example, agricultural commodities may exhibit seasonal price movements based on planting and harvesting cycles.

- *Calendar Spread Strategies:* Calendar spread strategies involve taking opposite positions in futures contracts with different expiration dates. Traders may aim to profit from changes in the price difference between the near-month and distant-month contracts.

How to Choose the Right Strategy

Selecting the right trading strategy depends on various factors, including:

- *Market Conditions:* Different strategies may perform better in specific market conditions. Trend following strategies may thrive in trending markets, while mean reversion strategies may be more suitable in range-bound markets.

- *Risk Tolerance:* Consider your risk tolerance and the level of exposure you are comfortable with. Some strategies, such as trend following, may involve holding positions for extended periods, while others, like day trading, require quick decision-making.

- *Market Knowledge:* The effectiveness of a strategy often depends on the trader's understanding of the specific commodity or market. Traders should choose strategies aligned with their expertise and the unique characteristics of the commodities they trade.

- *Time Commitment:* Different strategies require varying levels of time commitment. Day trading may demand constant monitoring of price movements, while longer-term strategies may allow for more flexibility.

In conclusion, mastering commodity trading involves selecting and implementing the right strategies based on market conditions, risk tolerance, and individual preferences. Traders should continuously refine and adapt their strategies as market dynamics evolve. In the subsequent chapters, we will explore advanced trading concepts and delve into the psychological aspects of successful commodity trading.

CHAPTER 9

TRADING PSYCHOLOGY

In the realm of commodity trading, technical expertise and market knowledge are undoubtedly crucial, but mastering the psychological aspects of trading is equally paramount. This chapter explores the intricate interplay between emotions and trading, the necessity of discipline and patience, strategies for developing a winning mindset, and the invaluable lessons derived from mistakes.

Emotions and Trading

The emotional roller coaster is an inherent part of trading. Fear, greed, excitement, and anxiety are emotions that can influence decision-making and impact trading outcomes. Recognizing and managing these emotions is vital for maintaining a rational and strategic approach to trading.

- *Fear:* Fear can lead to hesitation, causing traders to miss out on profitable opportunities or exit positions prematurely. It may also result in a reluctance to take calculated risks. Implementing risk management strategies and maintaining a rational perspective can help mitigate fear.

- *Greed:* Greed can lead to impulsive and irrational decisions, such as overtrading or holding onto winning positions for too long. Establishing clear profit-taking and exit strategies, along with setting realistic goals, can help curb the influence of greed.

- *Excitement and Overconfidence:* Experiencing success can generate excitement and overconfidence, leading to a lack of diligence in analyzing potential risks. Traders should remain vigilant, adhering to their strategies and avoiding complacency.

Discipline and Patience

Discipline and patience are the bedrock of successful trading. Following a well-defined trading plan and adhering to established rules are crucial components of discipline. Patience allows traders to wait for optimal entry and exit points, avoiding impulsive decisions driven by short-term market fluctuations.

- *Trading Plan:* A comprehensive trading plan outlines entry and exit criteria, risk management strategies, and the overall approach to trading. Following the plan diligently, even in the face of emotional impulses, is a hallmark of discipline.

- *Risk Management:* Disciplined risk management involves setting predefined risk levels for each trade and adhering to them rigorously. This includes using tools like stop-loss orders to limit potential losses.

- *Patience in Waiting for Opportunities:* Successful traders understand the importance of waiting for high-probability setups. Patience prevents premature entries or exits based on market noise and short-term fluctuations.

Developing a Winning Mindset

Developing a winning mindset involves cultivating psychological traits that contribute to long-term success in trading.

- *Adaptability:* Markets are dynamic and ever-changing. A winning mindset involves the ability to adapt to different market conditions, adjust strategies when necessary, and learn from both successes and failures.

- *Resilience:* Trading inevitably involves setbacks. A winning mindset is characterized by resilience— bouncing back from losses, learning from mistakes, and continuing to evolve as a trader.

- *Continuous Learning:* A growth-oriented mindset emphasizes continuous learning. Successful traders stay informed about market trends, explore new strategies, and seek to enhance their skills over time.

Learning from Mistakes

Mistakes are an inevitable part of trading, but the key lies in turning them into valuable learning experiences.

- *Analyzing Trades:* After a trade, it's crucial to conduct a thorough analysis, regardless of whether it resulted in a profit or a loss. Understanding what went well and identifying areas for improvement contributes to ongoing development.

- *Journaling:* Keeping a trading journal can be a powerful tool for learning from mistakes. Documenting trades, emotions, and decision-making processes provides a tangible record for self-reflection and improvement.

- *Adapting Strategies:* Recognizing when a strategy is not working and being willing to adapt is a hallmark of successful traders. The ability to pivot and refine approaches based on past experiences is crucial for sustained success.

Conclusion

Mastering trading psychology is an ongoing journey that involves self-awareness, discipline, and continuous improvement. Embracing the psychological aspects of trading and developing a resilient mindset are essential components of long-term success in the dynamic and challenging world of commodity trading. In the subsequent chapters, we will explore advanced trading concepts and provide insights into staying ahead in an ever-evolving market landscape.

CHAPTER 10

COMMODITY MARKET RESEARCH

In the fast-paced and ever-evolving world of commodity trading, staying well-informed is a cornerstone of success. This chapter delves into the essential components of effective commodity market research, including leveraging news sources and reports, utilizing historical data and analysis, conducting economic and political research, and staying ahead of market trends.

Staying Informed: News Sources and Reports

Timely and accurate information is a trader's most valuable asset. Keeping abreast of relevant news sources and reports is crucial for understanding the factors that influence commodity prices.

- *Financial News Outlets:* Mainstream financial news outlets provide real-time updates on global economic conditions, geopolitical events, and market trends. Websites, television channels, and financial publications can be valuable sources of information.

- *Government Reports:* Government agencies release reports that offer key insights into various commodities. For example, the U.S. Department of Agriculture (USDA) releases crop reports, while the Energy Information Administration (EIA) provides data on energy markets. These reports can have a significant impact on commodity prices.

- *Industry Reports:* Industry-specific reports, published by organizations or research firms, offer in-depth analyses of commodity markets. These reports can provide nuanced perspectives and valuable data for making informed trading decisions.

Historical Data and Analysis

Understanding historical data is fundamental to comprehending market trends, patterns, and potential future movements.

- *Price Charts:* Analyzing price charts provides a visual representation of historical price movements. Traders use charts to identify trends, support and resistance levels, and potential reversal patterns.

- *Technical Analysis:* Historical price data forms the basis of technical analysis. By studying past price movements and applying technical indicators, traders can identify patterns and trends that may repeat in the future.

- *Seasonal Patterns:* Historical data often reveals seasonal patterns in commodity markets. Understanding when certain commodities are historically more or less in demand can aid traders in anticipating price movements.

Economic and Political Research

Economic and political factors play a significant role in shaping commodity markets. Conducting thorough research in these areas is crucial for gaining insights into market dynamics.

- *Economic Indicators:* Monitoring economic indicators such as GDP growth, inflation rates, and employment figures provides a broader understanding of the economic environment. Changes in economic conditions can impact the demand for commodities.

- *Political Events:* Political decisions, trade policies, and geopolitical events can have profound effects on commodity markets. Traders should stay informed about political developments globally, as these can introduce volatility and uncertainty.

- *Interest Rates and Currency Movements:* Changes in interest rates and currency values can influence commodity prices. Understanding the interplay between monetary policies and commodity markets is essential for making informed trading decisions.

Staying Ahead of Market Trends

Staying ahead of market trends involves anticipating shifts in supply and demand dynamics, technological advancements, and broader economic trends.

- *Technological Developments:* Advances in technology can impact commodity markets, particularly in sectors like energy and metals. For example, innovations in renewable energy may influence the demand for traditional energy commodities.

- *Global Economic Trends:* Understanding global economic trends and anticipating shifts in consumer behavior can provide valuable insights into the future demand for commodities.

- *Supply Chain Analysis:* Examining the entire supply chain for a commodity, from production to distribution, can reveal potential bottlenecks or disruptions that may affect prices.

Conclusion

Effective commodity market research is a multifaceted endeavor that involves staying informed through news sources and reports, analyzing historical data, conducting economic and political research, and anticipating future trends. Traders who dedicate time and effort to comprehensive research are better positioned to make informed decisions and navigate the complexities of commodity markets successfully. In the subsequent chapters, we will explore advanced trading concepts and provide insights into optimizing trading strategies.

CHAPTER 11

TRADING SYSTEMS AND AUTOMATION

In the contemporary landscape of commodity trading, the integration of technology has revolutionized the way traders operate. This chapter explores the realm of trading systems and automation, encompassing algorithmic trading, trading software and platforms, the crucial processes of backtesting and optimization, and the implementation of effective risk management in automated trading.

Algorithmic Trading

Algorithmic trading involves the use of computer algorithms to execute trading strategies with speed and precision. Traders rely on algorithms to analyze market data, identify opportunities, and execute trades at optimal prices. Key components of algorithmic trading include:

- *Market Analysis:* Algorithms analyze vast amounts of market data, identifying patterns, trends, and potential trading opportunities.

- *Order Execution:* Algorithms swiftly execute trades according to predefined criteria, often in fractions of a second, minimizing the impact of market fluctuations.

- *High-Frequency Trading (HFT):* High-frequency trading is a subset of algorithmic trading characterized by exceptionally high trade execution speeds. HFT strategies capitalize on small price differentials and market inefficiencies.

Trading Software and Platforms

Sophisticated trading software and platforms provide traders with tools to execute strategies, analyze market data, and manage their portfolios. These platforms offer a range of features, including:

- *Real-time Market Data:* Access to up-to-the-second market data is crucial for making informed decisions. Trading platforms provide real-time quotes, charts, and news feeds.

- *Order Execution:* Efficient order execution is a hallmark of trading platforms. Traders can place, modify, and cancel orders with ease, utilizing various order types such as market orders, limit orders, and stop orders.

- *Technical Analysis Tools:* Robust trading platforms offer a suite of technical analysis tools, including charting capabilities, technical indicators, and drawing tools.

- *Risk Management Features:* Many platforms include risk management features such as stop-loss orders and position sizing tools to help traders manage their exposure effectively.

Backtesting and Optimization

Backtesting is the process of assessing the performance of a trading strategy using historical data. It allows traders to evaluate how a strategy would have performed in the past before applying it to live markets. Optimization involves fine-tuning a strategy to maximize its performance.

- *Benefits of Backtesting:* Backtesting provides insights into a strategy's strengths and weaknesses, helping traders refine their approaches. It allows for the identification of potential issues and the improvement of risk-adjusted returns.

- *Challenges of Backtesting:* While backtesting is a valuable tool, it comes with challenges. Overfitting, or tailoring a strategy too closely to historical data, can lead to poor performance in live markets. Traders must strike a balance between optimizing for historical data and ensuring robustness for future conditions.

Risk Management in Automated Trading

Effective risk management is critical in automated trading to safeguard against unexpected market events and algorithmic errors.

- *Position Sizing:* Determining the appropriate size for each position is a crucial aspect of risk management. Automated systems must incorporate position sizing rules to ensure that each trade aligns with the trader's risk tolerance.

- *Stop-Loss Mechanisms:* Implementing stop-loss mechanisms in automated trading systems helps limit potential losses. These mechanisms are triggered when a trade moves against the expected direction, automatically exiting the position to prevent further losses.

- *Diversification:* Automated trading systems may involve multiple strategies or instruments. Diversification across different markets or assets helps mitigate the impact of poor performance in a specific area.

- *Monitoring and Oversight:* Despite the automated nature of trading systems, ongoing monitoring and oversight are essential. Traders must regularly review performance, assess the impact of changes in market conditions, and intervene if necessary.

Conclusion

Trading systems and automation have reshaped the landscape of commodity trading, offering efficiency, speed, and precision. Algorithmic trading, supported by advanced software and platforms, has become integral to the industry. However, successful implementation requires thorough backtesting, optimization, and a robust risk management framework. In the subsequent chapters, we will explore advanced trading concepts and provide insights into optimizing trading strategies for sustained success in the dynamic world of commodity trading.

CHAPTER 12

COMMODITY MARKET ETHICS AND REGULATIONS

In the complex and interconnected world of commodity trading, ethics and regulations play a pivotal role in maintaining market integrity, protecting participants, and fostering fair and transparent practices. This chapter explores critical aspects of commodity market ethics and regulations, including the challenges posed by insider trading and market manipulation, the role of regulatory bodies and oversight mechanisms, the importance of compliance and reporting requirements, and the broader legal and ethical considerations that guide participants in these markets.

Insider Trading and Market Manipulation

Insider Trading: Insider trading involves trading securities based on material, non-public information. In the context of commodities, this could include confidential information about supply and demand dynamics, production levels, or other factors influencing prices. Insider trading undermines market fairness by giving certain participants an unfair advantage.

- *Consequences:* Insider trading is illegal and subject to severe penalties, including fines and imprisonment. It erodes market confidence and poses ethical concerns by exploiting information imbalances.

Market Manipulation: Market manipulation involves artificially inflating or deflating prices or creating a false appearance of market activity to deceive other participants. In commodity markets, manipulation can occur through spreading false information, cornering the market, or engaging in practices that distort supply and demand dynamics.

- *Regulatory Response:* Regulators actively monitor and investigate potential cases of market manipulation. Participants found guilty of market manipulation may face fines, civil penalties, and legal consequences.

Regulatory Bodies and Oversight

Commodity Futures Trading Commission (CFTC): In the United States, the Commodity Futures Trading Commission (CFTC) is a key regulatory body overseeing commodity markets. It regulates futures and options markets to ensure their integrity, transparency, and protection of market participants.

Securities and Exchange Commission (SEC): The SEC plays a crucial role in regulating securities markets, including some commodity-related securities. It works to maintain fair and efficient markets, facilitate capital formation, and protect investors.

International Regulatory Bodies: Commodity markets are global, and international bodies, such as the International Organization of Securities Commissions (IOSCO), collaborate to establish common standards and principles for market regulation.

Compliance and Reporting Requirements

Compliance Programs: Market participants, including traders, brokers, and firms, are required to establish and maintain compliance programs. These programs ensure adherence to applicable laws, regulations, and ethical standards. They often include training, monitoring, and reporting mechanisms.

Transaction Reporting: Participants in commodity markets must comply with transaction reporting requirements. This involves accurately and promptly reporting details of their trades to regulatory authorities. Transparent reporting contributes to market oversight and helps detect irregularities.

Legal and Ethical Considerations

Fair Dealing: Market participants are expected to engage in fair dealing. This includes honest and transparent communication, avoiding deceptive practices, and treating all participants equitably.

Conflicts of Interest: Managing conflicts of interest is crucial in maintaining market integrity. Participants must disclose potential conflicts and take measures to ensure that their actions do not compromise fair and unbiased market practices.

Compliance with Laws: Adhering to all applicable laws and regulations is a fundamental ethical consideration. This includes both domestic and international regulations that govern commodity markets.

Social Responsibility: Participants in commodity markets are increasingly expected to consider social and environmental responsibilities. Sustainable and ethical practices contribute to long-term market stability and resilience.

Conclusion

Commodity market ethics and regulations are essential pillars that sustain fair, transparent, and efficient trading environments. Insider trading, market manipulation, and other unethical practices not only violate the law but also erode the trust and credibility of commodity markets. Traders, brokers, and firms must remain vigilant, uphold ethical standards, and comply with regulations to contribute to the overall health and integrity of commodity markets. In the subsequent chapters, we will explore advanced trading concepts and provide insights into optimizing trading strategies within the framework of ethical and regulatory considerations.

CHAPTER 13

COMMODITY MARKET STRATEGIES FOR BEGINNERS

Embarking on the journey of commodity trading as a beginner can be both exciting and challenging. This chapter is dedicated to guiding newcomers in the world of commodity markets, covering essential strategies and practices to build a strong foundation for successful trading.

Getting Started with a Simulated Account

Before diving into live trading, beginners should consider using a simulated or demo account. This allows for hands-on experience with real market conditions without risking actual capital.

- *Benefits of Simulated Trading:*

- **Risk-Free Environment:** Simulated accounts enable traders to practice strategies and hone their skills without the fear of financial loss.

- **Familiarization with Platforms:** Beginners can become accustomed to trading platforms, order types, and other tools without real money at stake.

- **Strategy Testing:** It provides an opportunity to test various trading strategies in a controlled environment.

Paper Trading and Building Experience

Once comfortable with simulated trading, transitioning to paper trading involves using a simulated environment but with a more realistic approach.

- *Paper Trading Objectives:*

  - **Risk Management Practice:** Traders can implement and refine risk management strategies.

  - **Execution Skills:** Practice executing trades efficiently and promptly.

  - **Market Analysis:** Develop skills in analyzing market trends, news, and other factors influencing commodity prices.

Creating a Trading Plan

A well-thought-out trading plan is a cornerstone for success in commodity trading. It serves as a roadmap, outlining a trader's goals, risk tolerance, and strategies.

- *Components of a Trading Plan:*

    - **Financial Goals:** Clearly define short-term and long-term financial objectives.

    - **Risk Tolerance:** Determine the level of risk acceptable for each trade and overall portfolio.

    - **Trading Strategies:** Specify the types of commodities to trade, timeframes, and preferred analysis methods (fundamental or technical).

    - **Position Sizing:** Outline how much capital to allocate to each trade.

    - **Exit Strategies:** Define criteria for taking profits or cutting losses.

Selecting Your First Trades

When selecting the first trades as a beginner, focus on simplicity and manageability.

- *Start with Few Commodities:* Begin with a small selection of commodities. This allows for better understanding and monitoring of market dynamics.

- *Leverage Simple Strategies:* Initially, employ straightforward strategies. For example, consider trend-following or mean-reversion strategies.

- *Diversify Thoughtfully:* Diversification helps spread risk. However, beginners should start with a manageable number of commodities to closely track and analyze.

Continuous Learning and Adaptation

The journey of a beginner in commodity trading is a continuous learning process. Stay informed about market trends, economic indicators, and global events. Be open to adapting strategies based on experience and market conditions.

Conclusion

Commodity trading for beginners involves a gradual and structured approach. Starting with simulated and paper trading builds the necessary skills and confidence before risking real capital. Crafting a solid trading plan and selecting initial trades thoughtfully sets the stage for a sustainable and successful trading journey. In the subsequent chapters, we will explore advanced trading concepts and provide insights into optimizing trading strategies for long-term success in commodity markets.

CHAPTER 14

ADVANCED TRADING STRATEGIES

As traders gain experience and confidence in commodity markets, they often explore more advanced trading strategies to optimize returns and manage risks. This chapter delves into advanced trading techniques, including scalping and day trading, swing trading and position trading, options and derivatives strategies, and the application of quantitative analysis.

Scalping and Day Trading

Scalping: Scalping is a high-frequency trading strategy focused on making small profits from minor price fluctuations. Traders executing scalping strategies aim to capitalize on short-term market inefficiencies.

- *Key Characteristics:*

- **Quick Trades:** Positions are opened and closed within minutes or seconds.

- **Small Profits:** Each trade aims for a small profit, which accumulates over numerous transactions.

- **Intense Monitoring:** Scalpers closely monitor real-time data and market depth.

Day Trading: Day trading involves opening and closing positions within the same trading day. Day traders seek to profit from intraday price movements and avoid overnight exposure.

- *Key Characteristics:*

  - **Intraday Timeframe:** All positions are closed before the market closes.

  - **Technical Analysis:** Day traders often rely on technical analysis and chart patterns.

  - **Leverage:** Day traders may use leverage to amplify returns within the intraday timeframe.

Swing Trading and Position Trading

Swing Trading: Swing trading aims to capture "swings" or price movements within an established trend. This strategy typically spans a few days to weeks.

- *Key Characteristics:*

- **Trend Identification:** Swing traders analyze trends and enter positions at potential reversal points.

- **Short to Medium-Term:** Positions are held for a few days to weeks.

- **Combination of Technical and Fundamental Analysis:** Both technical and fundamental factors may influence swing trading decisions.

Position Trading: Position trading takes a longer-term approach, with positions held for weeks, months, or even years. Traders focus on fundamental analysis and macroeconomic trends.

- *Key Characteristics:*

  - **Fundamental Analysis:** In-depth analysis of supply and demand factors, economic indicators, and geopolitical events.

  - **Long-Term Trend Following:** Positions are aligned with major, long-term trends.

  - **Lower Trade Frequency:** Position traders make fewer trades, allowing for a more hands-off approach.

Options and Derivatives Strategies

Options Strategies: Options provide traders with the right, but not the obligation, to buy or sell an asset at a predetermined price. Advanced options strategies include:

- **Straddles and Strangles:** Simultaneously buying a call and a put option (straddle) or out-of-the-money call and put options (strangle) to profit from significant price movements.

- **Iron Condors:** Combining a bull put spread and a bear call spread to profit from low volatility and limited price movements.

Derivatives Strategies: Beyond options, traders may explore various derivative strategies using futures and other financial instruments.

- **Arbitrage:** Exploiting price differences between related assets on different exchanges to make a risk-free profit.

- **Spread Trading:** Simultaneously buying and selling related contracts to profit from price differentials.

Quantitative Analysis

Quantitative analysis involves using mathematical models, statistical techniques, and algorithms to analyze market data and identify trading opportunities.

- *Algorithmic Trading:* Implementing pre-programmed algorithms to execute trades based on predefined criteria.

- *Statistical Arbitrage:* Identifying mispricings in related assets and taking advantage of statistical relationships.

Risk Management in Advanced Strategies

While advanced strategies can offer enhanced opportunities, they also come with increased complexity and risk. Robust risk management is essential to mitigate potential downsides.

- *Advanced Order Types:* Utilizing advanced order types, such as stop-limit orders, to manage risk more precisely.

- *Portfolio Diversification:* Diversifying across different strategies and asset classes to spread risk.

Conclusion

Advanced trading strategies open up new possibilities for experienced traders in commodity markets. Whether adopting short-term techniques like scalping or day trading, exploring medium-term strategies like swing trading, delving into derivatives, or applying quantitative analysis, a thorough understanding of the chosen strategy and diligent risk management are imperative. In the subsequent chapters, we will further explore advanced concepts and provide insights into navigating the complexities of commodity markets.

CHAPTER 15

CASE STUDIES AND REAL-LIFE EXAMPLES

Real-life examples and case studies provide invaluable insights into the dynamic and unpredictable nature of commodity markets. This chapter explores successful commodity traders, examines notable market crashes and recoveries, draws lessons from historical events, and analyzes recent trends to offer practical wisdom for traders navigating the complexities of these markets.

Successful Commodity Traders

Paul Tudor Jones: Renowned for predicting the 1987 stock market crash, Paul Tudor Jones is a successful hedge fund manager and commodity trader. His focus on macroeconomic analysis and understanding the broader market environment contributed to his success.

Louise Yamada: As a technical analyst, Louise Yamada has made significant contributions to the field. Her ability to identify long-term trends and reversals has earned her recognition as one of the most successful technical analysts in the financial industry.

Jim Rogers: An advocate for commodities as an investment class, Jim Rogers co-founded the Quantum Fund with George Soros. Rogers' emphasis on long-term trends and the global economic landscape has shaped his successful career as a commodity trader.

Notable Market Crashes and Recoveries

The 2008 Financial Crisis: The 2008 financial crisis had a profound impact on commodity markets. As global markets experienced a severe downturn, commodity prices plummeted. However, commodities played a role in the recovery, with increased demand from emerging markets contributing to their resurgence.

The Oil Price Collapse in 2014: The sudden drop in oil prices in 2014, driven by oversupply and weakening demand, had far-reaching effects on commodity markets. This event highlighted the interconnectedness of global markets and the impact of geopolitical factors on commodity prices.

Lessons from Historical Events

Lessons from the Great Depression: The Great Depression of the 1930s significantly impacted commodity markets. The importance of understanding macroeconomic factors, the role of government policies, and the resilience of certain commodities during economic downturns are enduring lessons from this period.

The Hunt Brothers' Silver Manipulation: The attempt by the Hunt brothers to corner the silver market in the late 1970s resulted in a spectacular market crash. This event underscored the risks of market manipulation and the need for robust regulatory oversight.

Analyzing Recent Trends

Renewable Energy Boom: The growing focus on renewable energy has reshaped commodity markets. Increased demand for metals like lithium, cobalt, and rare earth elements reflects the shift toward renewable technologies, presenting new opportunities for commodity traders.

Technology and Commodities: Advancements in technology, such as blockchain and artificial intelligence, have introduced innovative ways of trading commodities. These technologies enhance transparency, efficiency, and risk management in commodity markets.

Conclusion

Real-life examples and case studies offer a wealth of knowledge for commodity traders. Studying successful traders provides insights into the strategies and approaches that contribute to long-term success. Analyzing market crashes and recoveries and drawing lessons from historical events equips traders with a deeper understanding of the complexities inherent in commodity markets. Additionally, staying abreast of recent trends, such as the renewable energy boom and technological advancements, positions traders to capitalize on emerging opportunities. In the subsequent chapters, we will continue to explore advanced concepts and provide practical guidance for navigating the ever-evolving landscape of commodity trading.

CHAPTER 16

THE FUTURE OF COMMODITY MARKETS

The landscape of commodity markets is continuously evolving, shaped by a myriad of factors ranging from technological advancements to shifts in global economic dynamics. This chapter explores the potential future scenarios for commodity markets, considering evolving market dynamics, the growing importance of sustainability and Environmental, Social, and Governance (ESG) factors, technological advancements, and the impact of globalization on emerging markets.

Evolving Market Dynamics

Shifts in Supply and Demand: Evolving patterns in supply and demand will continue to influence commodity markets.

Factors such as population growth, urbanization, and changing consumer preferences will impact the demand for various commodities. Additionally, geopolitical events, climate change, and technological disruptions can alter supply dynamics.

Renewable Energy Transition: The global transition towards renewable energy sources is a defining trend in commodity markets. As societies move away from traditional fossil fuels, there will be increased demand for metals like lithium, cobalt, and rare earth elements, crucial components of renewable technologies.

Innovation in Agriculture: In agriculture, technological innovations, precision farming, and advancements in crop genetics are likely to reshape the sector. These innovations can impact the supply of agricultural commodities and influence trading strategies.

Sustainability and ESG Factors

ESG Investing: The rise of Environmental, Social, and Governance (ESG) investing has significant implications for commodity markets. Investors are increasingly considering sustainability criteria when making investment decisions, influencing the demand for commodities produced through environmentally and socially responsible practices.

Carbon Markets: The development of carbon markets and the integration of carbon pricing mechanisms can impact commodities. Industries may face increased pressure to reduce carbon emissions, influencing production processes and affecting the prices of carbon-intensive commodities.

Technological Advancements

Blockchain and Smart Contracts: Technological advancements, particularly blockchain technology, can enhance transparency and efficiency in commodity markets. The use of smart contracts can streamline trade processes, reduce fraud, and provide a more secure and transparent trading environment.

Artificial Intelligence (AI) and Data Analytics: AI and data analytics are transforming how traders analyze information and make decisions. Predictive analytics, machine learning models, and algorithms can process vast amounts of data, providing traders with valuable insights and potentially enhancing trading strategies.

Globalization and Emerging Markets

Rise of Emerging Markets: The economic growth of emerging markets, particularly in Asia and Africa, is reshaping global commodity markets. Increased industrialization, urbanization, and rising middle-class populations in these regions contribute to growing demand for commodities.

Impact of Trade Policies: Globalization and shifts in trade policies can influence commodity markets. Trade tensions, tariffs, and geopolitical events have the potential to disrupt supply chains and impact the prices of traded commodities.

Conclusion

The future of commodity markets is dynamic and multifaceted. Evolving market dynamics, sustainability considerations, technological advancements, and the rise of emerging markets are key factors shaping the trajectory of these markets. Traders and market participants need to adapt to changing conditions, leverage technological innovations, and consider the broader impact of sustainability and ESG factors on commodity investments. Navigating the future of commodity markets requires a holistic understanding of these interconnected factors and the ability to seize emerging opportunities in a rapidly changing landscape. In the subsequent chapters, we will delve deeper into specific aspects of commodity trading, providing insights and strategies to empower traders in this dynamic environment.

CHAPTER 17

CONCLUSION AND RECAP

As we conclude this comprehensive exploration of commodity markets, it's essential to recap key takeaways, reflect on the journey covered, and offer some final thoughts to guide you in your ongoing pursuit of success in commodity trading.

Key Takeaways

1. **Diverse Commodity Landscape:**

   - Commodity markets encompass a wide array of assets, including energy, metals, agricultural products, and financial instruments. Understanding the unique characteristics of each commodity is fundamental to successful trading.

2. **Market Fundamentals:**

   - Supply and demand dynamics, geopolitical events, economic indicators, and weather conditions significantly impact commodity prices. Traders must stay informed about these fundamental factors to make informed decisions.

3. **Trading Strategies:**

   - From fundamental and technical analysis to advanced strategies like scalping, day trading, and options trading, a diverse toolkit of strategies is crucial. The choice of strategy should align with your risk tolerance, time horizon, and market conditions.

4. **Risk Management:**

   - Effective risk management is a cornerstone of successful commodity trading. Establishing a clear trading plan, setting risk limits, and employing risk mitigation tools such as stop-loss orders are essential for protecting capital.

5. **Technological Integration:**

   - Embracing technological advancements, including algorithmic trading, blockchain, and artificial intelligence, can enhance efficiency, transparency, and decision-making in commodity trading.

6. **Ethics and Regulations:**

- Adhering to ethical standards and regulatory compliance is non-negotiable in commodity trading. Understanding and navigating the legal landscape ensures market integrity and investor protection.

7. **Continuous Learning:**

- Commodity markets are dynamic, and continuous learning is crucial for staying ahead. Keeping abreast of market trends, exploring new strategies, and adapting to evolving conditions are essential for long-term success.

The Journey Ahead

The journey in commodity trading is a dynamic and ever-evolving process. As you move forward, consider the following:

1. **Adaptability:**

- Markets change, and the ability to adapt is paramount. Stay flexible in your approach, be open to new strategies, and embrace change as an opportunity for growth.

2. **Continuous Improvement:**

- Complacency is the enemy of progress. Commit to continuous improvement by analyzing past trades, learning from mistakes, and staying curious about new developments in commodity markets.

3. **Global Perspective:**

   - Commodity markets are global, and a broad understanding of global economic trends, geopolitical events, and emerging market dynamics will provide a comprehensive perspective.

Final Thoughts

Commodity trading is a challenging yet rewarding endeavor that demands a combination of skill, discipline, and resilience. As you navigate the complexities of these markets, remember:

- **Patience and Discipline:**

  - Markets can be unpredictable, and success often requires patience and discipline. Stick to your trading plan, manage risks diligently, and avoid impulsive decisions.

- **Continuous Learning:**

  - The world of commodity trading is dynamic, with new opportunities and challenges arising regularly. Embrace a mindset of continuous learning, stay curious, and remain adaptable to change.

- **Community and Networking:**

    - Engage with the trading community, whether online or through local networks. Learning from others, sharing experiences, and building a supportive network can be invaluable in your trading journey.

In conclusion, the world of commodity trading offers a vast and dynamic landscape for exploration. Armed with knowledge, strategic acumen, and a commitment to continuous improvement, you are well-positioned to navigate the complexities of commodity markets. May your journey be marked by success, resilience, and a passion for the ever-evolving world of commodities. Happy trading!

APPENDIX A

GLOSSARY OF COMMODITY MARKET TERMS

Commodity markets are filled with specialized terminology essential for understanding the intricacies of trading and investing. This glossary serves as a comprehensive reference guide to key terms used in commodity markets.

Agricultural Commodities:

1. **Grains:** Crops such as wheat, corn, soybeans, and rice.

2. **Softs:** Commodities like coffee, cocoa, sugar, and cotton.

Basis: The difference between the local cash price of a commodity and the price of the nearest futures contract for the same or a related commodity.

Bear Market: A market characterized by declining prices, pessimism, and a general lack of confidence among investors.

Bull Market: A market characterized by rising prices, optimism, and a general confidence among investors.

Contango: A situation in which the futures price of a commodity is higher than the spot price.

Derivative: A financial contract whose value is derived from the performance of an underlying asset, index, or rate.

Exchange-Traded Fund (ETF): A type of investment fund and exchange-traded product, with shares that trade on stock exchanges.

Futures Contract: A standardized financial contract to buy or sell a specified quantity of an underlying asset at a predetermined price at a specified time in the future.

Hedging: Using financial instruments, such as futures contracts, to offset the risk of adverse price movements in the cash market.

Inflation Hedge: An investment that is expected to protect against the erosion of purchasing power caused by inflation.

Leverage: The use of various financial instruments or borrowed capital to increase the potential return of an investment.

Margin: The amount of money or collateral deposited by a trader with their broker when opening a futures position.

Option: A financial contract that gives the buyer the right, but not the obligation, to buy or sell an asset at a predetermined price before or at the expiration date.

Pip: In currency trading, a pip is a unit of movement in the exchange rate of a currency pair.

Quantitative Easing: A monetary policy in which a central bank buys financial assets to increase the money supply and encourage lending and investment.

Roll Yield: The profit or loss generated by rolling a futures contract from one expiration to another.

Short Selling: Selling an asset with the expectation that its price will decline, allowing the seller to buy it back at a lower price.

Technical Analysis: An approach to evaluating securities by analyzing statistics generated by market activity, such as historical prices and trading volume.

Underlying Asset: The financial instrument upon which a derivative's price is based.

Volatility: A statistical measure of the dispersion of returns for a given security or market index.

Warrant: A financial instrument giving the holder the right, but not the obligation, to buy or sell an underlying asset at a specified price before or at the expiration date.

XAU: The symbol for gold, often used in financial markets to represent the price of gold.

Yield: The income return on an investment, usually expressed as an annual percentage.

Zero-Sum Game: A situation in which one participant's gain or loss is exactly balanced by the losses or gains of other participants.

This glossary provides a foundation for understanding the language of commodity markets. As you delve into the complexities of trading and investing, refer to this glossary to enhance your comprehension of key terms.

APPENDIX B

RECOMMENDED READING AND RESOURCES

For those seeking to deepen their understanding of commodity markets and enhance their trading skills, the following list comprises recommended reading and resources. These books, websites, and educational platforms cover a range of topics, from market fundamentals to advanced trading strategies.

Books:

1. **"A Random Walk Down Wall Street" by Burton Malkiel:**

   - A classic guide covering various investment strategies, including insights into commodities and their role in a diversified portfolio.

2. **"Reminiscences of a Stock Operator" by Edwin Lefèvre:**

   - Although focused on stocks, this timeless book provides valuable lessons in trading psychology and market dynamics applicable to commodities.

3. **"Hot Commodities" by Jim Rogers:**

   - Written by a legendary commodity investor, this book offers insights into the historical trends and future potential of various commodities.

4. **"Market Wizards" by Jack D. Schwager:**

   - A collection of interviews with successful traders, offering diverse perspectives and trading wisdom applicable to commodity markets.

5. **"Technical Analysis of the Financial Markets" by John J. Murphy:**

   - A comprehensive guide to technical analysis, covering chart patterns, indicators, and strategies relevant to commodity trading.

6. **"The Intelligent Investor" by Benjamin Graham:**

- A foundational work on value investing, emphasizing principles applicable to commodities and the broader financial markets.

Websites and Platforms:

1. **Investopedia (**www.investopedia.com**):**

   - A comprehensive online resource covering financial topics, including detailed explanations of commodity market concepts.

2. **Commodity Research Bureau (**www.crbtrader.com**):**

   - A valuable source for commodity market research, providing historical data, analysis, and market insights.

3. **Bloomberg Commodity Index (**www.bloomberg.com/markets/commodities**):**

   - Access real-time data, news, and analysis on a wide range of commodities, including energy, metals, and agriculture.

4. **CME Group Education (**www.cmegroup.com/education**):**

   - The educational portal of CME Group offers resources, webinars, and courses on futures and options trading.

5. **TradingView (**www.tradingview.com**):**

   - A platform for charting and technical analysis, allowing users to analyze and share trading ideas across various markets, including commodities.

Educational Platforms:

1. **Coursera (**www.coursera.org**):**

   - Explore online courses on finance, trading, and commodity markets offered by top universities and institutions.

2. **Udemy (**www.udemy.com**):**

   - A platform with a wide array of courses on trading strategies, technical analysis, and commodities.

3. **Khan Academy (**www.khanacademy.org**):**

   - Khan Academy offers free courses on economics and finance, providing a solid foundation for understanding market dynamics.

4. **LinkedIn Learning (**www.linkedin.com/learning**):**

   - Access courses on trading, risk management, and financial analysis, enhancing your skills in commodity markets.

Financial News and Analysis:

1. **Bloomberg (**www.bloomberg.com**):**

   - A global source for financial news, data, and analysis, covering a wide range of commodities and markets.

2. **Financial Times (**www.ft.com**):**

   - A reputable source for global business and financial news, offering in-depth coverage of commodity markets.

3. **The Wall Street Journal (**www.wsj.com**):**

   - A leading financial newspaper providing comprehensive coverage of global markets, including commodities.

Forums and Communities:

1. **Elite Trader (**www.elitetrader.com**):**

   - An online community for traders to share insights, strategies, and discuss market trends, including commodities.

2. **Reddit - Commodities (**www.reddit.com/r/commodities**):**

   - Join discussions on commodity markets, news, and trading strategies with a community of traders and enthusiasts.

Conclusion:

Continuous learning is integral to success in commodity trading. Explore these resources, stay informed about market trends, and engage with the trading community to broaden your knowledge and refine your skills. The ever-evolving nature of commodity markets demands a commitment to ongoing education and a willingness to adapt to new insights and strategies.

APPENDIX C

SAMPLE TRADING PLANS AND STRATEGIES

A well-structured trading plan is crucial for success in commodity markets. This appendix provides sample trading plans and strategies that can serve as templates for developing your personalized approach. Remember to tailor these samples to your risk tolerance, market understanding, and individual goals.

Sample Trading Plan

1. Trading Goals:

- Define short-term and long-term financial objectives.

- Specify the desired percentage return on investment.

2. Risk Tolerance:

- Determine the maximum acceptable risk per trade and overall portfolio risk.

- Establish stop-loss levels based on technical or fundamental factors.

3. Asset Allocation:

- Allocate a specific percentage of capital to different commodities or sectors.

- Diversify across energy, metals, agriculture, and financial instruments.

4. Trading Timeframe:

- Identify the preferred trading timeframe (e.g., day trading, swing trading, position trading).

- Align trading strategies with the chosen timeframe.

5. Trading Strategies:

- Include a mix of fundamental and technical analysis.

- Specify the criteria for entering and exiting trades.

- Incorporate both trend-following and mean-reversion strategies.

6. Position Sizing:

- Determine the size of each position based on risk tolerance and overall portfolio size.

- Utilize the 1-2% rule for position sizing to manage risk effectively.

7. Exit Strategies:

- Define criteria for taking profits and cutting losses.

- Incorporate trailing stops and profit targets.

8. Market Analysis:

- Stay informed about macroeconomic trends, geopolitical events, and supply-demand dynamics.

- Utilize both historical data and real-time information for analysis.

9. Record Keeping:

- Maintain a detailed trading journal documenting each trade.

- Analyze and review trades regularly to identify strengths and weaknesses.

10. Continuous Learning:

- Commit to ongoing education through courses, books, and market research.

- Stay updated on new market trends and trading strategies.

Sample Trading Strategy: Trend Following in Energy Markets

1. Objective:

- Capitalize on established trends in the energy sector for short to medium-term gains.

2. Timeframe:

- Swing trading with a focus on weekly and daily charts.

3. Asset Selection:

- Target major energy commodities such as crude oil and natural gas.

4. Entry Criteria:

- Enter long positions when the commodity is in an uptrend, confirmed by moving averages and trendline analysis.

- Enter short positions when a clear downtrend is identified.

5. Exit Criteria:

- Exit long positions when signs of trend reversal or overbought conditions appear.

- Exit short positions when signs of trend reversal or oversold conditions appear.

6. Risk Management:

- Set stop-loss orders based on a percentage of the average true range (ATR).

- Use position sizing to limit risk to 1-2% of the total trading capital per trade.

7. Additional Filters:

- Consider fundamental factors such as geopolitical events and supply-demand reports.

- Use technical indicators like the Relative Strength Index (RSI) to confirm trend strength.

8. Review and Adjust:

- Regularly review the performance of the strategy.

- Adjust parameters based on evolving market conditions and lessons learned.

These samples provide a framework for structuring your trading plans and strategies. Customize them based on your unique preferences, risk tolerance, and market insights. Regularly evaluate and refine your plans to adapt to changing market conditions and enhance your overall trading performance.

www.ingramcontent.com/pod-product-compliance
Lightning Source LLC
Chambersburg PA
CBHW062335290526
45794CB00005B/2040